DARYL TALBOT'S COWBOY CARTOONS #3

OTHER BOOKS BY DARYL TALBOT:

COWBOY CARTOONS
COWBOY CARTOONS, TOO

DARYL TALBOT'S
COWBOY
CARTOONS
#3

A FIREBIRD PRESS BOOK

PELICAN PUBLISHING COMPANY
Gretna 1998

First Pelican edition, 1996

*The word "Pelican" and the depiction of a pelican are trademarks of Pelican
Publishing Company, Inc., and are registered
in the U.S. Patent and Trademark Office.*

Library of Congress Cataloging-in-Publication Data

Talbot, Daryl.
  [Cowboy cartoons #3]
  Daryl Talbot's cowboy cartoons #3—1st Pelican ed.
   p. cm.
  ISBN 1-56554-223-1 (pb : alk. paper)
  1. Cowboys—Caricatures and cartoons. 2. American wit and
humor, Pictorial. I. Title.
  NC1429.T16A4 1996
  741.5'973—dc20   96-19277
                                          CIP

Manufactured in the United States of America
Published by Pelican Publishing Company, Inc.
1000 Burmaster Street, Gretna, Louisiana 70053

To my sons, Kenny and Kevin

Acknowledgments

Most of the cartoons on the following pages have appeared in *Western Horseman, Western Horse, Cowboy Sports News, The Circuit News, Super Looper, Northeast Reining Horse Association Directory,* and numerous rodeo, ranch rodeo, and roping publications. My thanks and appreciation to those publications and to the many Western and rodeo friends across the country for their support and encouragement.

DARYL TALBOT'S COWBOY CARTOONS #3

ONCE MORE! "A" AS IN APPALOOSA, "B" AS IN BUCKSKIN...

HARDER, SIS! SEE
IF YOU CAN **THROW** ME!

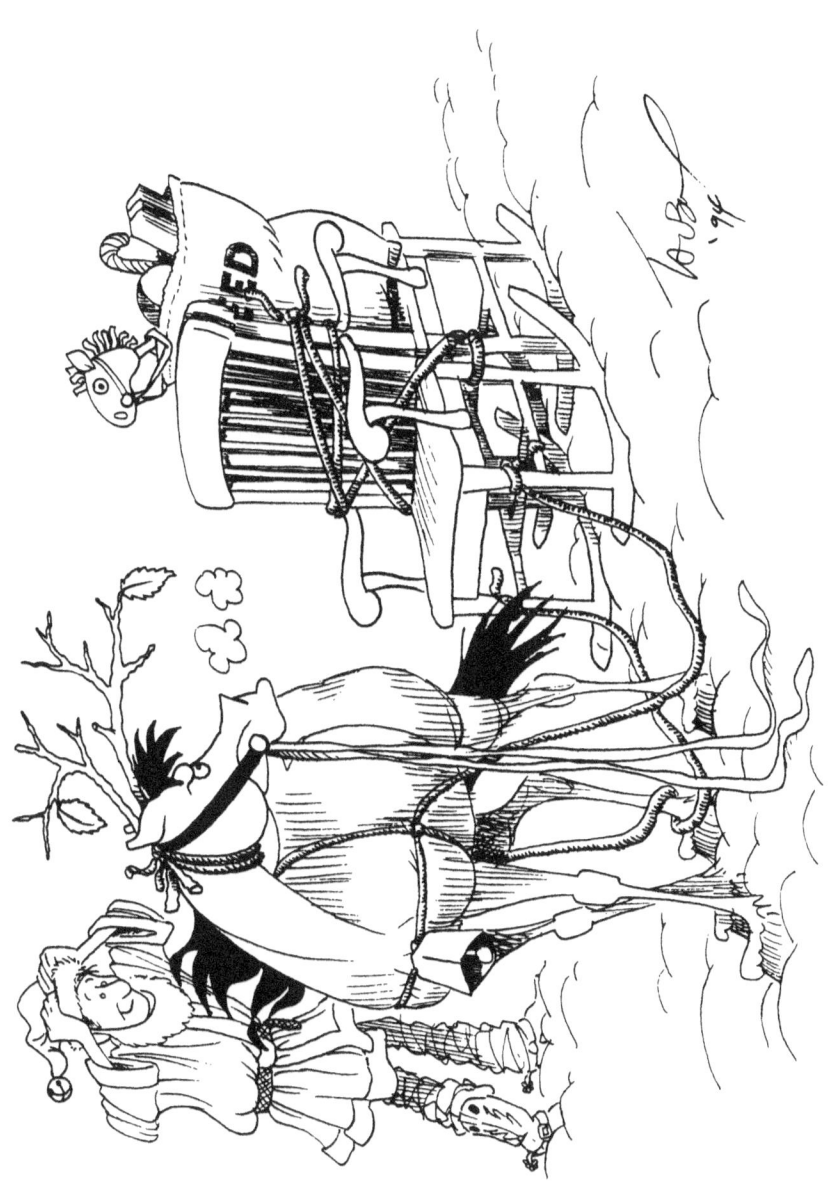

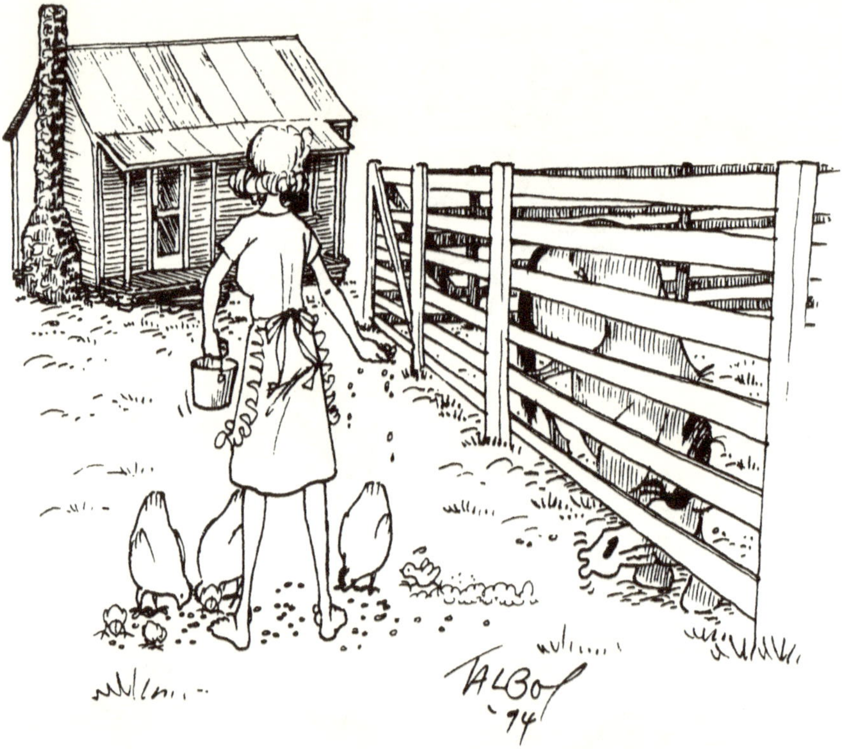
TALBOT
'94

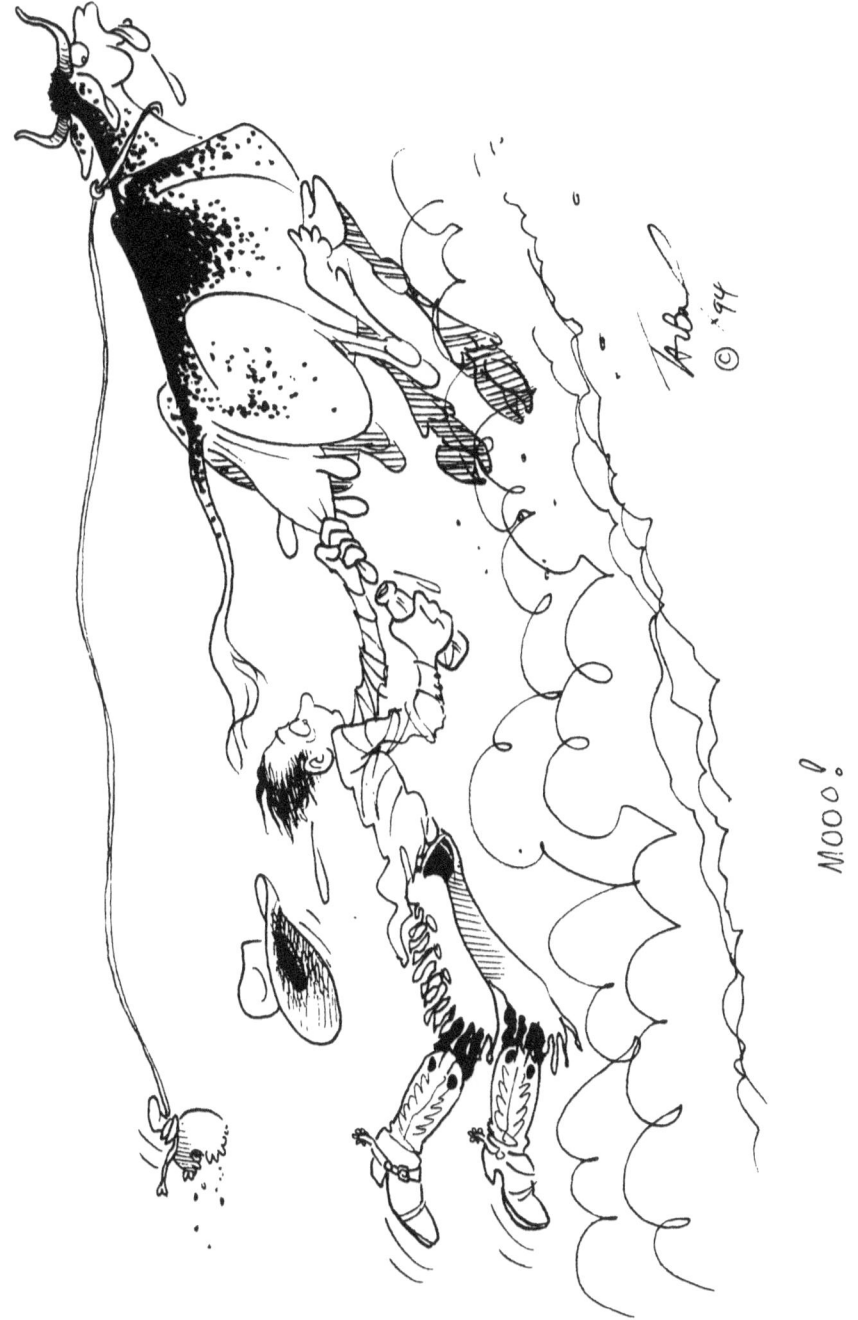

Mooo!

ONLY THREE! ONLY THREE!

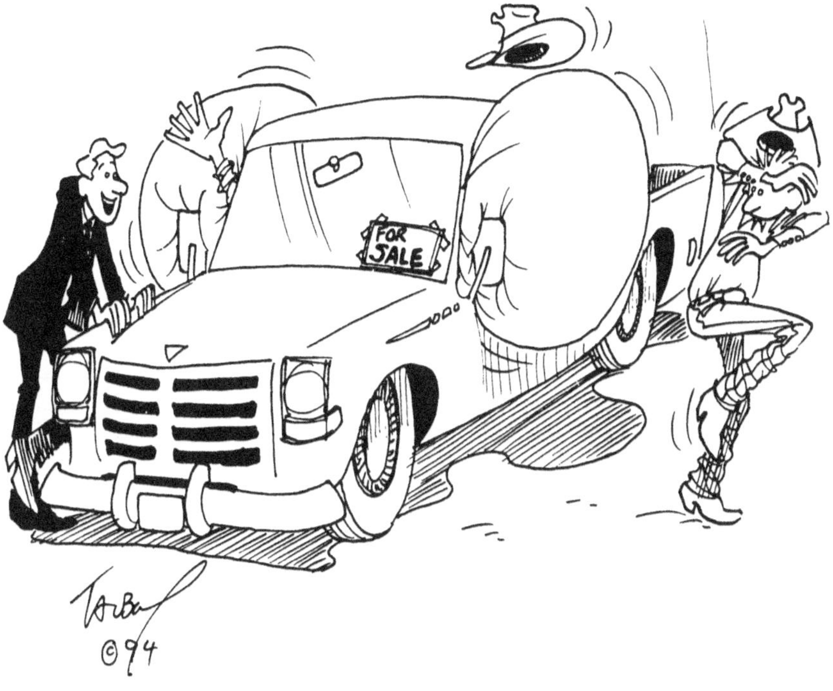
FOR SALE
©94

... AND LAST, BUT NOT LEAST, IT HAS ONE **OVER-SIZED** AIRBAG THAT PROTECTS EVERYONE!

GRANDPA! GRANDMA'S *FLIRTIN'* WITH THE COWBOYS AGAIN!

IT'S A **COWBOY RECLINER!** IT **VIBRATES** AT A **WALK, LOPE** AND **GALLOP.**

IN QUIRING MINDS WANT TO KNOW !

DALLY! DALLY! DALLY!

THAT WAS A 1ST PLACE RUN! THANKS, MOM!

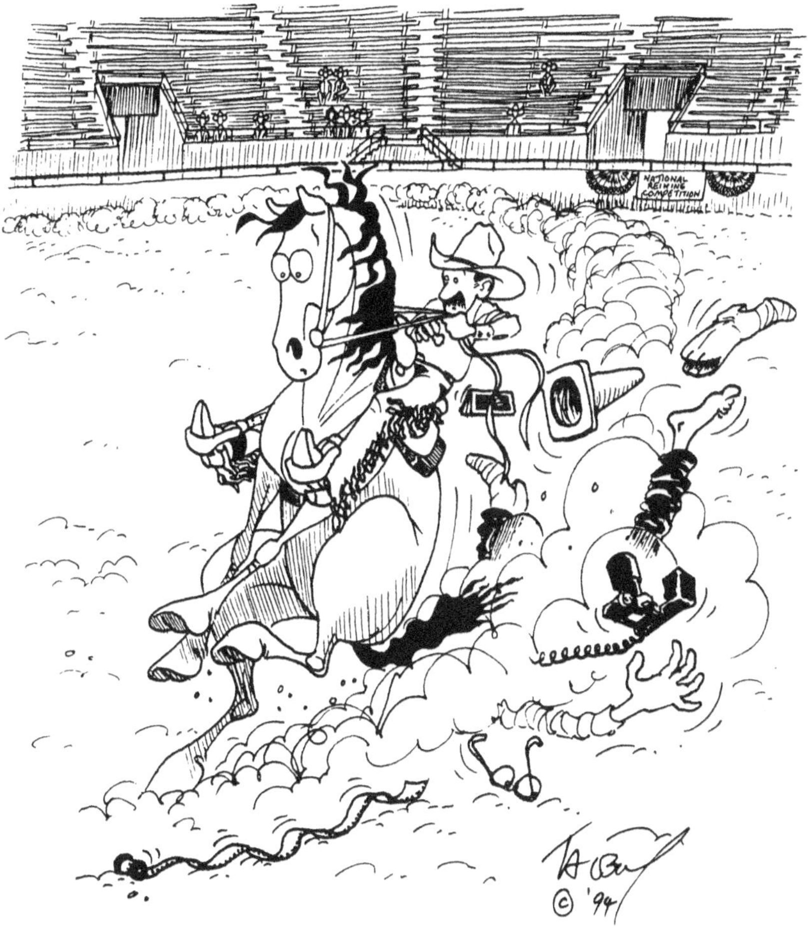
NATIONAL REINING COMPETITION
© '94

ROOKIE!

NOW, THAT'S A PRIME EXAMPLE OF WHY **DOG** IS MAN'S **BEST FRIEND!**

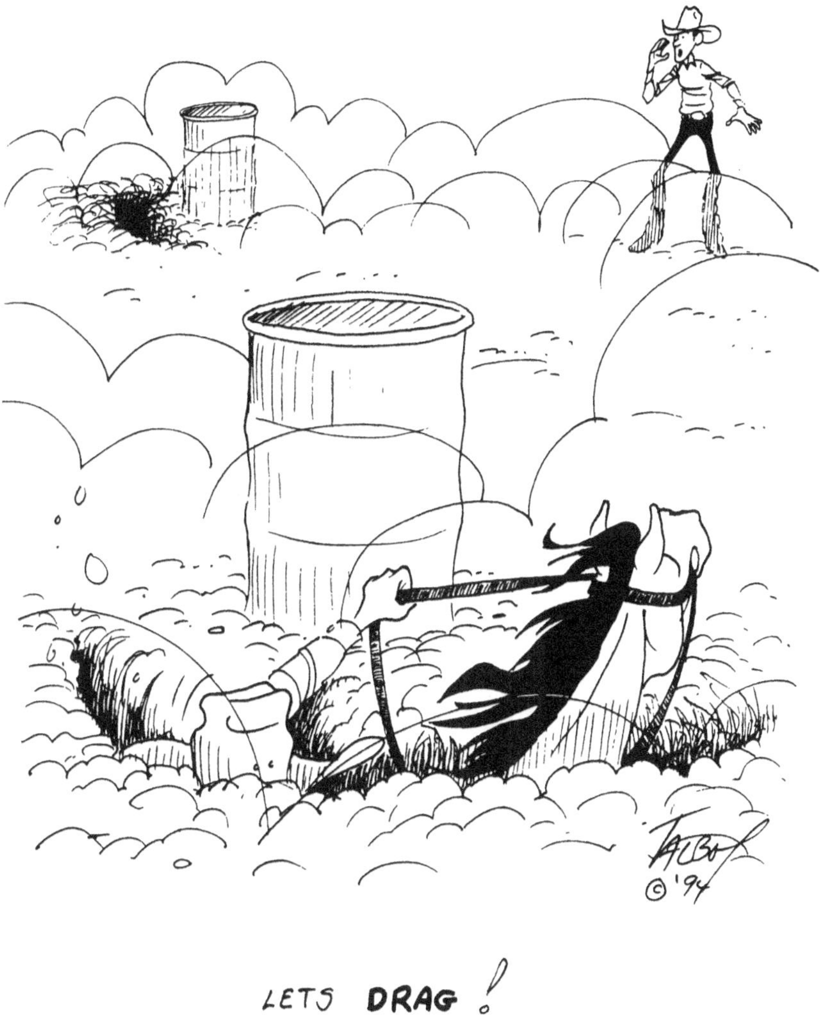
©'94

LETS **DRAG** !

UH... AND THE CONTESTANT VOTED MOST
CONGENIAL IS... UH... MISS **PISTOL** ANNIE!

SO MUCH FOR YOUR **COWBOY LOGIC**!

JUST BECAUSE **I** FOUND YOUR SOCKS AND **YOU** COULDN'T DOESN'T MEAN THE BEDROOM'S **HAUNTED**!

LETS **CALL IN** SICK THIS MORNIN'!

PA, FORGET CHANGIN' THAT **FLAT TIRE** AND COME ON!

HEY! NO HOLDIN' ALLOWED IN CUTTIN' COMPETITIONS!

WITH THOSE **JINGLE-BOB SPURS**,
WE CAN HEAR HIM COMING
IN TIME TO **HIDE**!

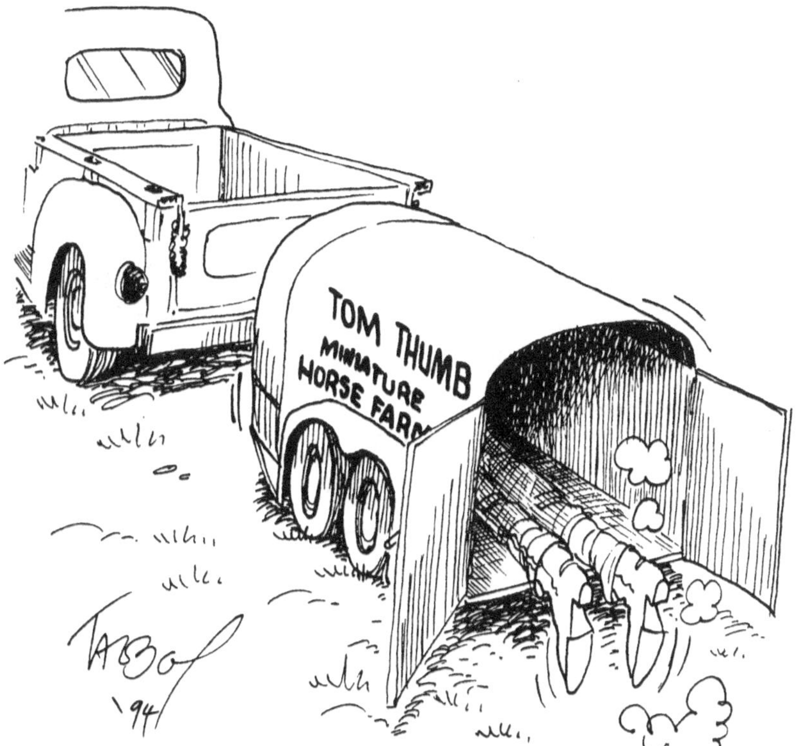
TOM THUMB
MINIATURE
HORSE FAR

WHOA!

TROUBLE! HE WEARS RANGE CUBES AROUND HIS NECK FOR GOOD LUCK... AND JUST LOST 'EM!

COWBOYIN'S MY **HOBBY**! I'M REALLY A **BRAIN SURGEON**!

HOW COULD YOU **POSSIBLY** FALL
OVER? YOU HAVE **FOUR LEGS**!

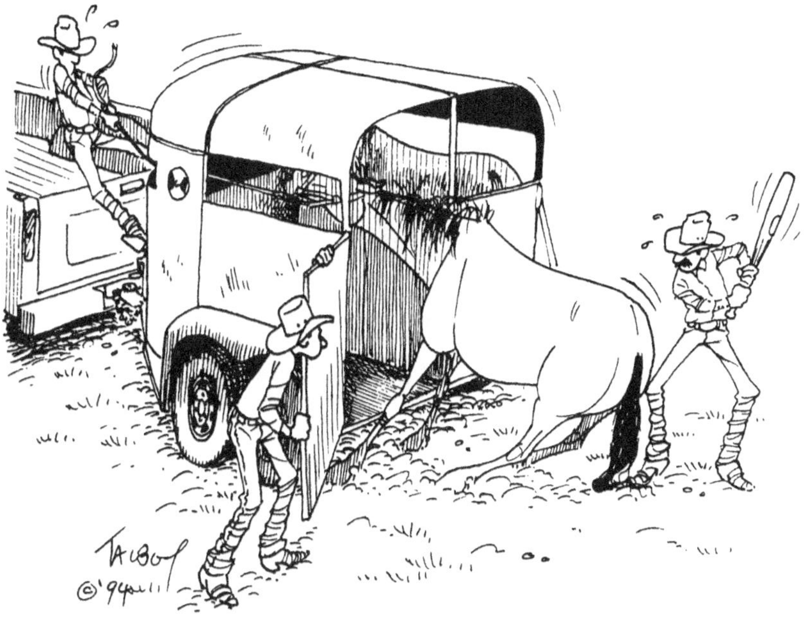
TALBOT
©'94

BATTER UP!

LOOKS LIKE WE HAVE A NEW **LEAD TIME** IN OUR **TEAM PENNING** COMPETITION!

IMPROVISE AND OVER COME!

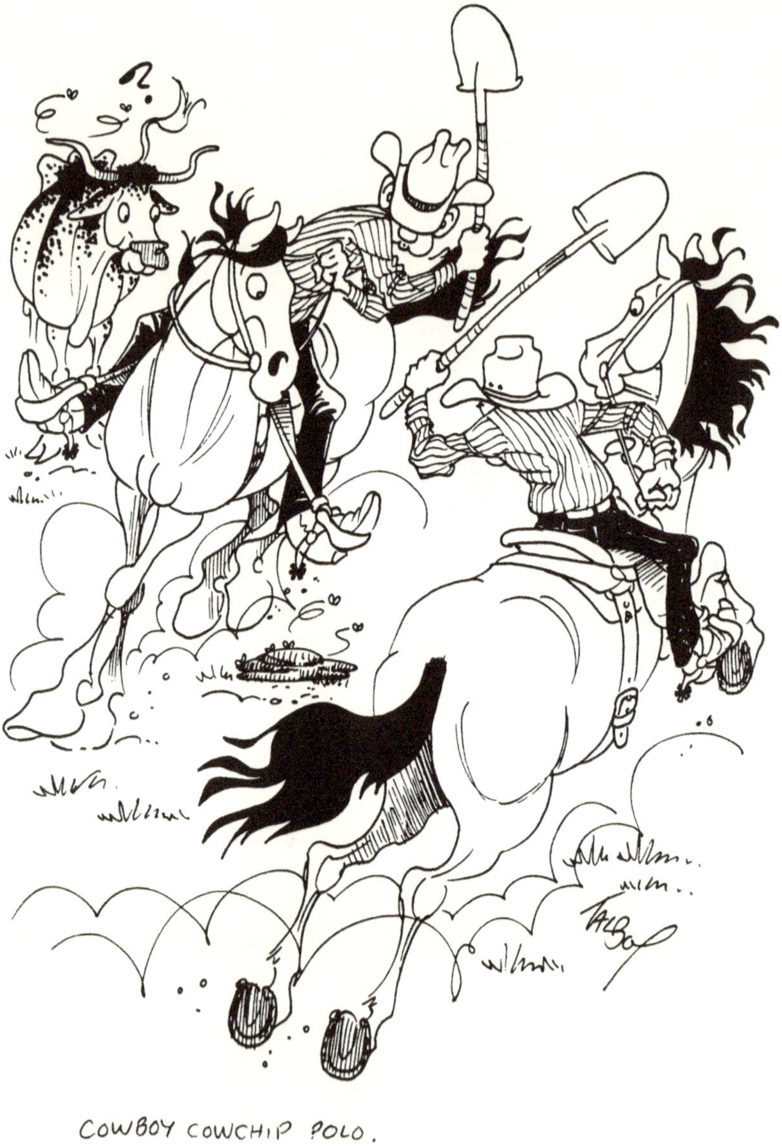

COWBOY COWCHIP POLO.

THERE, BUT FOR THE GRACE OF GOD, GO I !

SLIM, WHAT'S THE **SMALLEST** LINE OF **BRANDS** YOU CAN READ?

... AND SHE'S EASY TO LOAD!

WHAT'S THE **PENALTY** FOR **UP-CHUCKIN'**?

ENTRY NUMBER 27, THE **JUDGES** WOULD LIKE A **WORD** WITH YOU.

DON'T THAT **BEAT ALL**? WE'RE A
DOIN' **CHORES** FOR **SPORT**!

GIVE IT UP, LARRY! YOU DONE **MISSED** YOUR STEER!

THERE'S A COUPLE OF **DRAWBACKS** TO HAVIN' A **GOOD** COOK.

YOU DON'T **HAVE** TO SEE 'EM!
LISTEN FOR THE **CHING** OF THEIR
SPURS AND **AIM** YOUR KICK AT
THE SOUND!

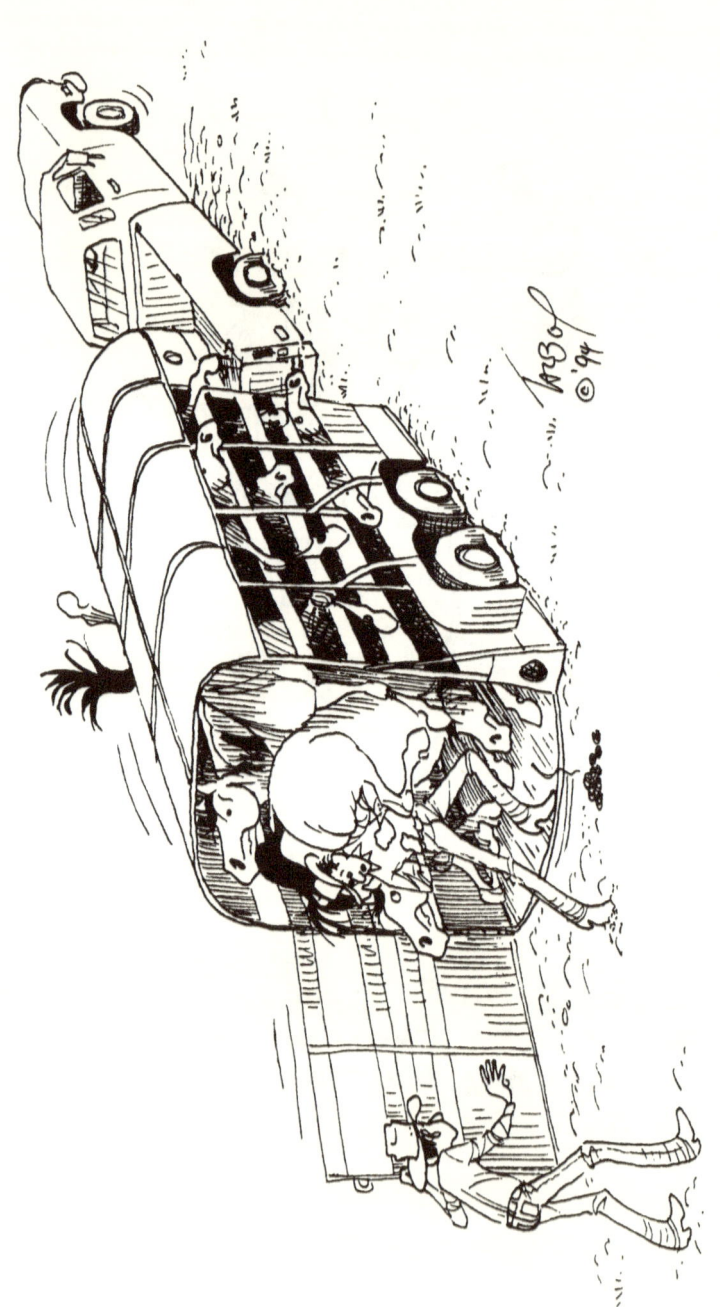

... BUT IT'LL HOLD A LOT MORE 'N THAT AND YOU DON'T HAVE TO MAKE AS MANY TRIPS!

WHY COULDN'T YOU'VE BEEN **BORN** A HORSE?

I DON'T HAVE A **MUSTACHE**... IT'S
MY **NOSE HAIRS**!

OKAY, COWBOY! WHERE'S THE **ROPIN'**!

MAN! I FEEL LIKE I'VE BEEN
RODE HARD AND PUT UP **WET!**

SOMEHOW I DON'T THINK WE'RE THE **FIRST** WHITEMEN THEY'VE SEEN. THAT'S A **CHARGECARD**!

HE REALLY AIN'T **CLUMSY**, JUS' SOME FOOL **FARRIER** PUT THE SHOES ON THE **WRONG** FEET!

THIS IS MY CHAUFFEUR!

SO MUCH FOR **YOUR** SHORT CUT!

THIS **PICTURE** IS SUPPOSE TO BE **SERIOUS!** SO, STOP **MAKIN' FACES!**

I HAVE TO REMEMBER TO KEEP MY **SPEED** DOWN, OTHERWISE IT'S **TOO HARD** FOR MA TO GET **DINNER** OFF THE GRILL! YA HUNGRY?

HAPPY BIRTHDAY, SON! THE FAMILY
TRUCK IS NOW **ALL** YOURS!

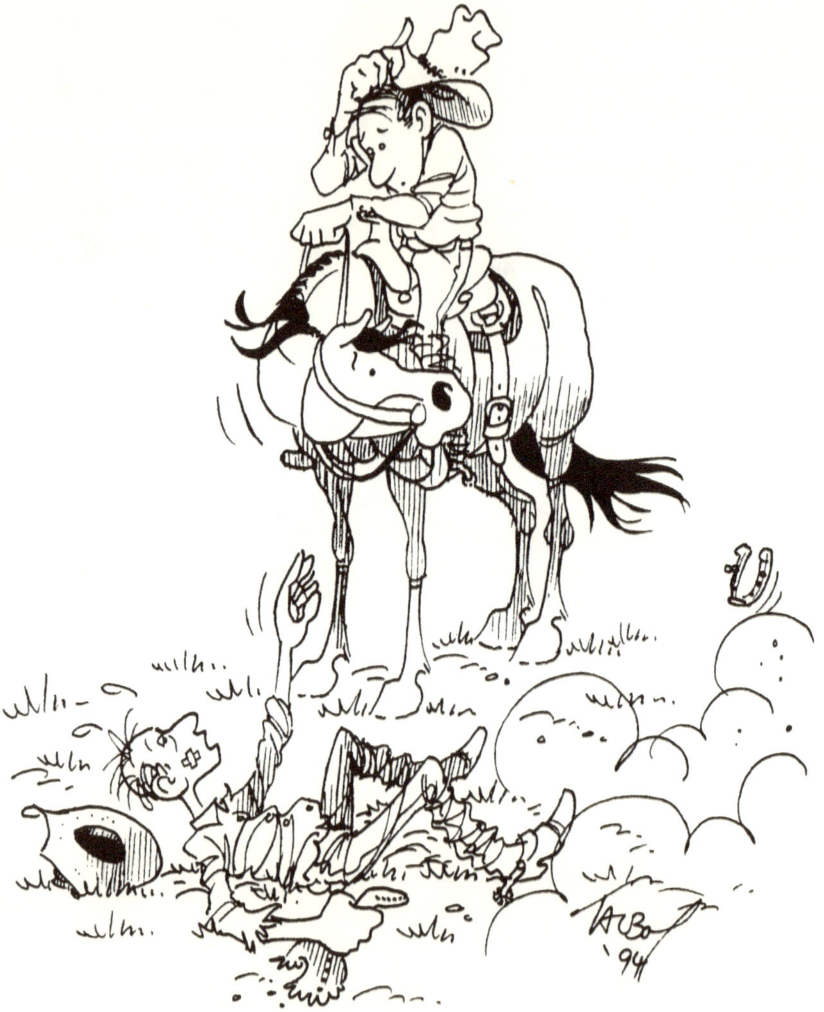

YOU WANT TO **BUY** A... HORSE?

SAY! THAT HORSE IS A REAL **BIT AND SPUR** COLLECTOR!

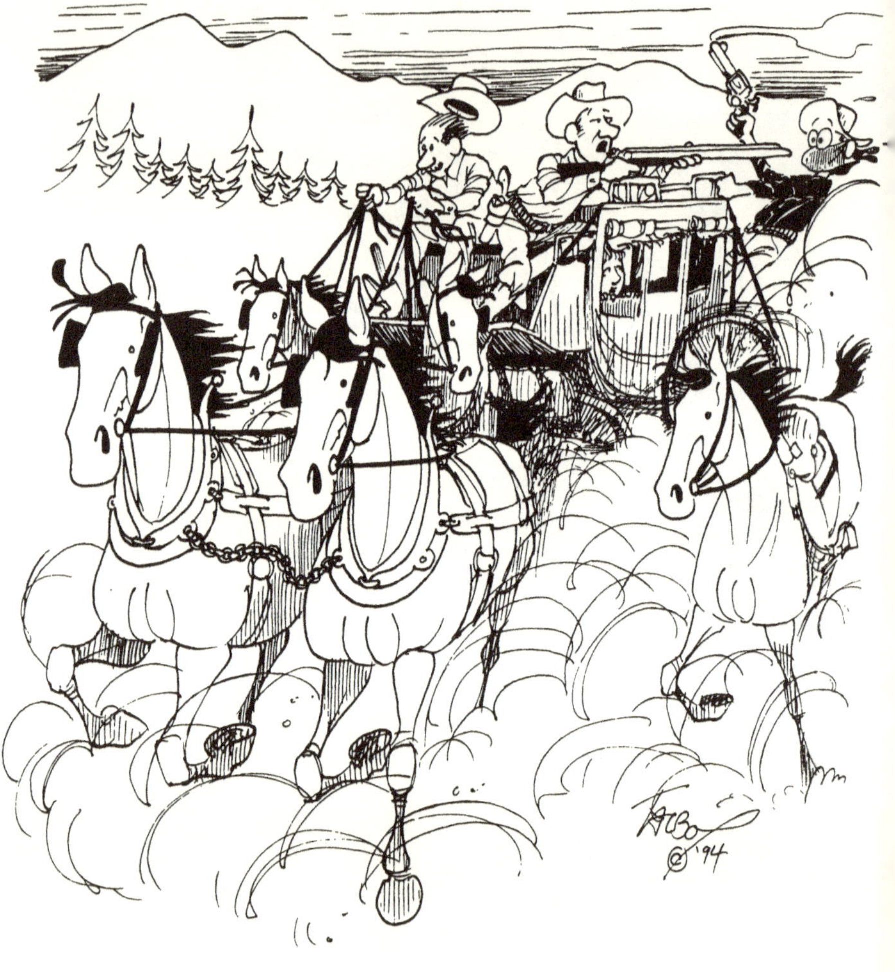

TICKET PLEASE!

ON SECOND THOUGHT... THE GRASS IS **GREENER** ON **THIS** SIDE OF AN **ELECTRIC FENCE**!

HE AIN'T **TOUGH**! HE'S JUST TOO **DUMB** TO SKIN IT FOR A **HATBAND**!

IF I **SLOW DOWN** WE'LL NEVER GET DONE BEFORE **DARK**!

I DON'T THINK HE REALIZES THAT IT'S **WAY PAST** MY BED TIME *!*

I'LL BET THIS IS THE FIRST TIME YOU'VE **CLEANED** STABLES!

BEGIN ON LEFT LEAD! KEEP YOUR ARM UP!
NOW, DO A RIGHT ROLLBACK! SMILE! STOP
AND DO FOUR SPINS! SMILE! DO A SLIDIN'
STOP! YOUR HAIR'S IN MY FACE! DO....

BACK SEAT REINER!

THE **REAL** REASON THE BUFFALO **DISAPPEARED** WAS BECAUSE THEY DIDN'T HAVE GOOD **ROPIN' HORNS**!

I'VE TIED OFF THIS **BAD TOOTH** HARD AND FAST AND I'M A GETTIN' **RID** OF IT!

ON THE **BRIGHT SIDE**! THE CATTLE CAN'T **STAMPEDE** IF THEY'RE **HOLDIN'** THEIR EARS!

WELL, WE **WOULD** HAVE MADE IT IF MY ROPE HADN'T **BROKE**!

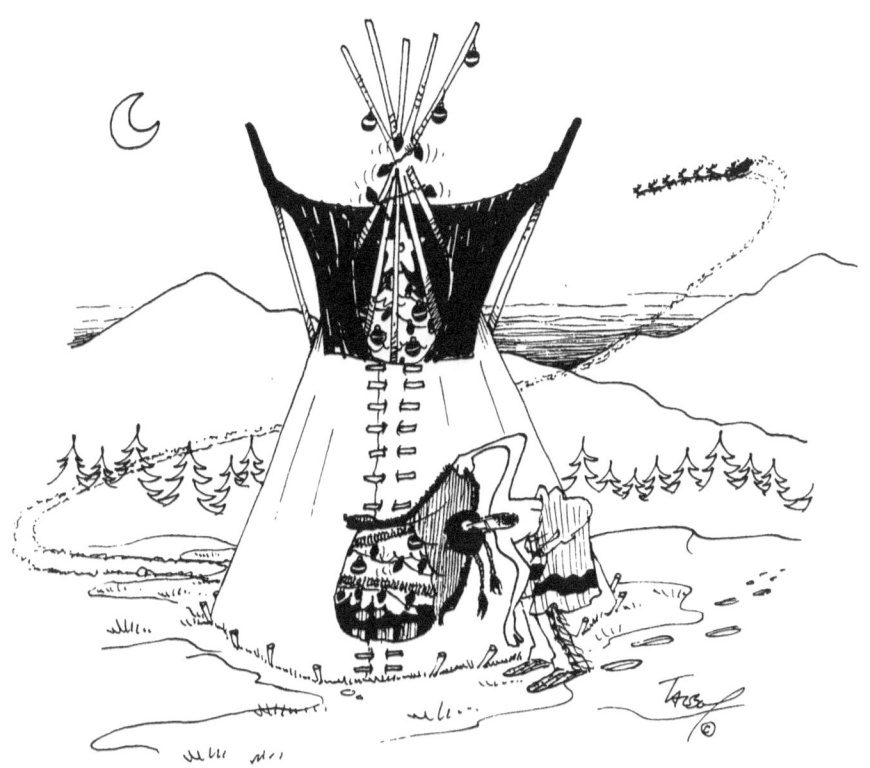

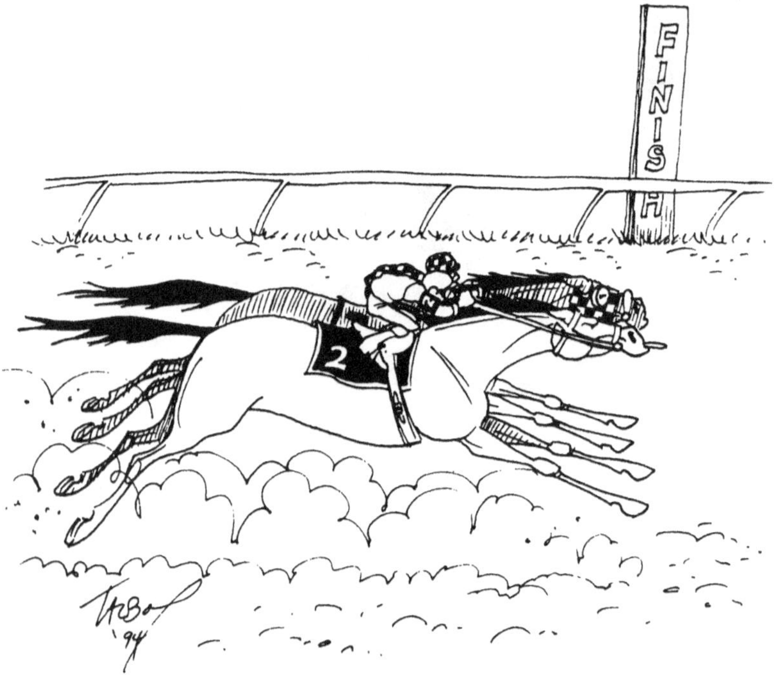
FINISH
2

THAT'S WHAT **COWBOYS** LOOK LIKE
BEFORE THEY'RE **WEANED**!

JUST DON'T **COMPROMISE** UNTIL
THIS LAUNDRY'S DRY!

CANNIBAL!

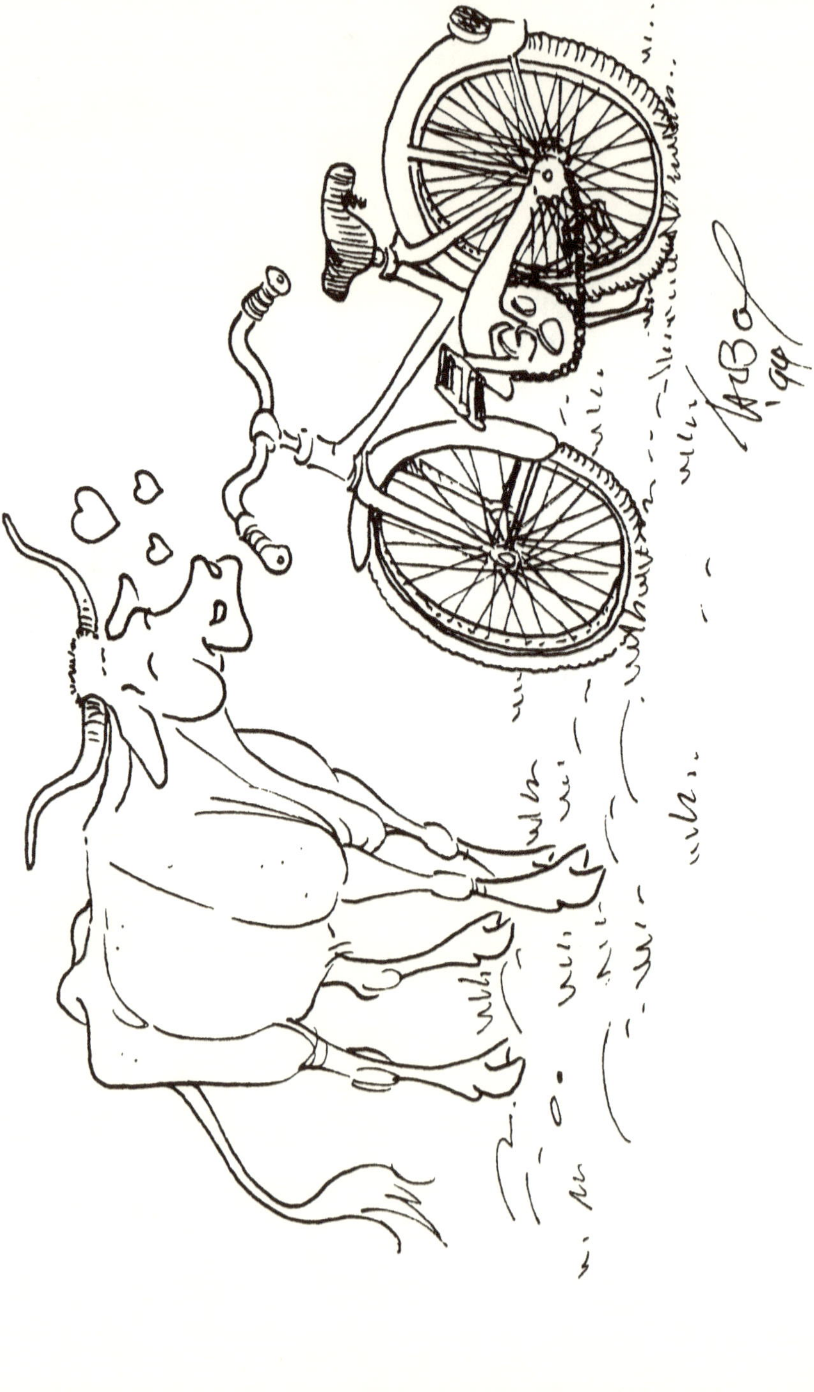

WELL, DAUGHTER. I BELIEVE YOU'VE FINALLY **OUTGROWN** OL' ROCKET!

...EIGHT... IT'S EIGHT SECONDS! IT'S EIGHT SECONDS!

IF **YOUR** DRIVIN', I AIN'T GOIN'!

MERRY CHRISTMAS! HERE'S THAT NEW SADDLE YOU WANTED... SOME ASSEMBLY REQUIRED!

WHY HURRY? IF I GET **DONE**
THE MISSES WILL JUS' HAVE ME DO
SOMETHIN' ELSE!

HE CALLS IT A **ZEBCO** SPIN!

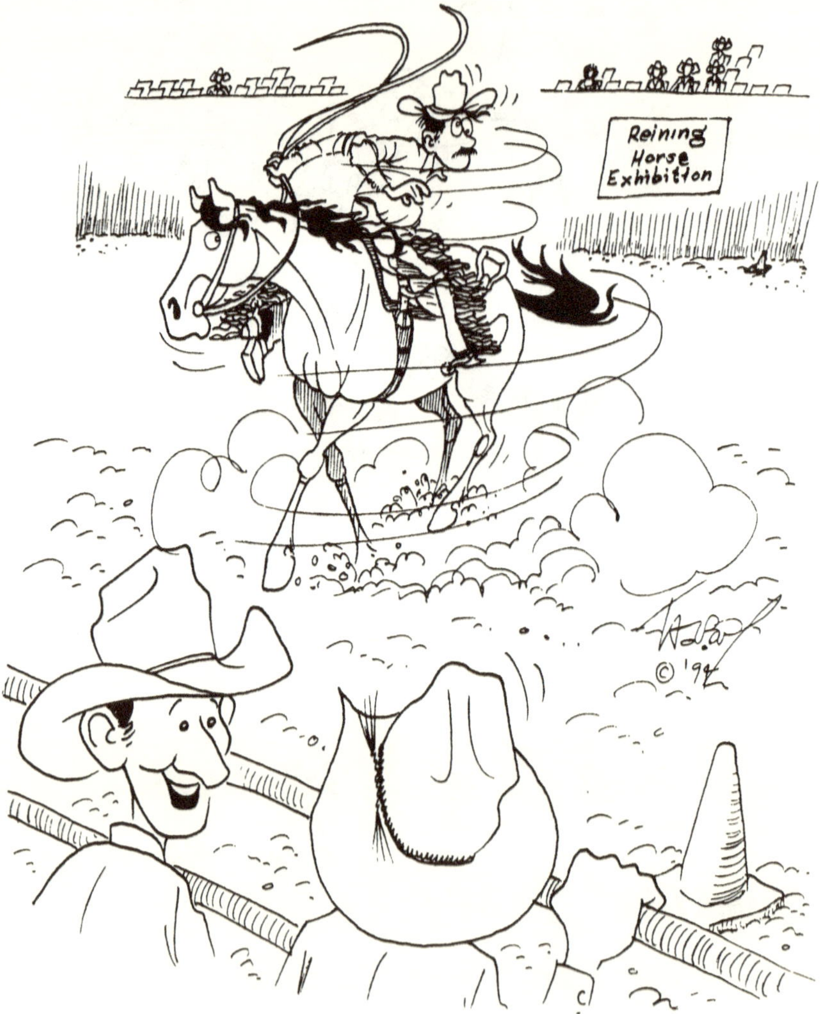
Reining
Horse
Exhibition

SAY, FRED! THERE'S A STIFF **FINE** FOR **LITTERIN'** IN THESE PARTS!

DO YOU KNOW HOW **LONG** A CRICKET LIVES? **ALL** NIGHT! **THAT'S** HOW LONG!

EVER' NOW AN' THEN I HAVE TO PUT THAT LITTLE **UPSTART** IN HIS PLACE!

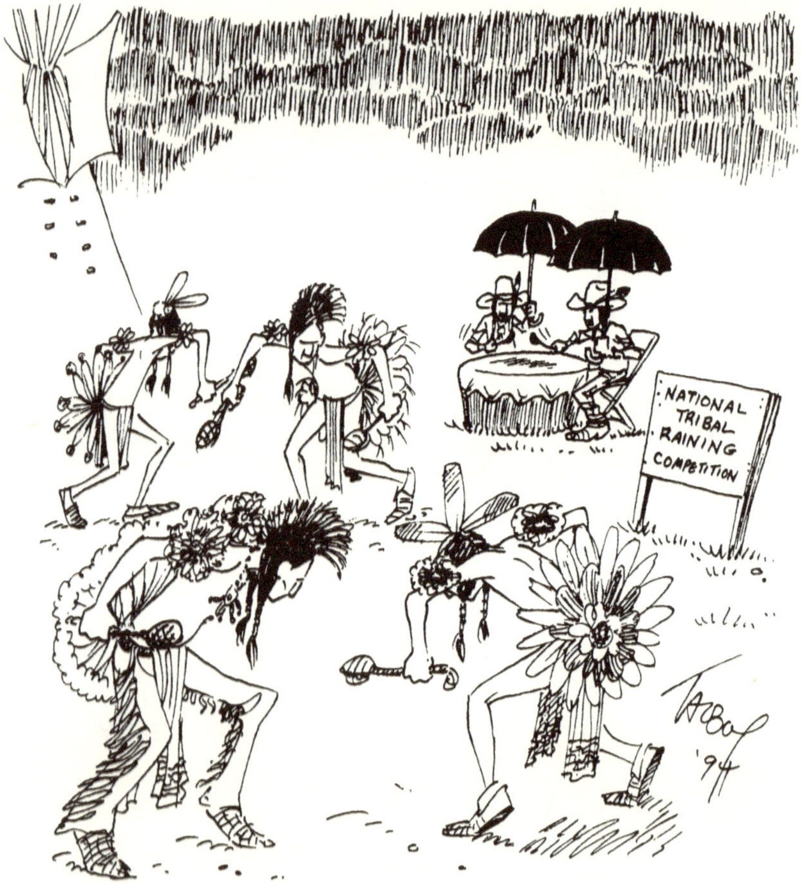
NATIONAL
TRIBAL
RAINING
COMPETITION
Talbot '94

THAT AWAY ? I THOUGHT WE WAS
A GOIN' **THIS** AWAY !

JUS' **HOW FER** IS THIS TARGET?

GET THE **CLOWN**! PASS THE WORD!

THIS CANOE 'LL HOLD FOUR MEN... **MEN**! YOU **FLATLANDER**!

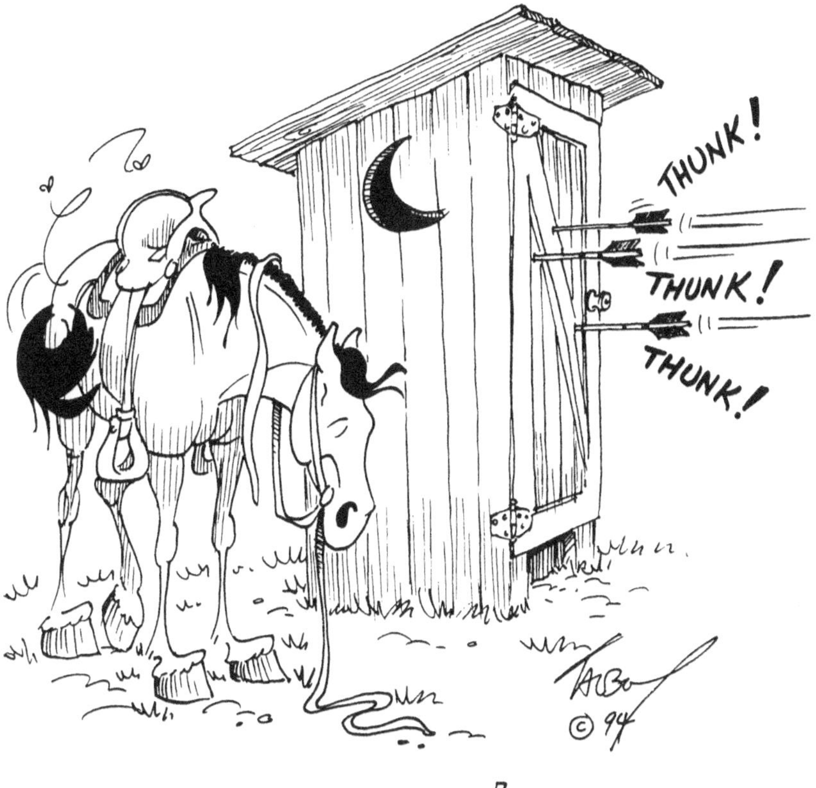
THUNK!
THUNK!
THUNK!
© 94

JUST A MINUTE!

CAN I HELP YA'LL?

HE'S **HALF** QUARTER HORSE, **HALF** ARABIAN, **HALF** MORGAN, **HALF** TEXAS WALKER AND **ALL** MINE!

BUT, SWEETHEART, YOUR **FREQUENT** CALLS OF NATURE IS GOIN' TO GET US **SNOWED-IN** AT THE PASS!

NOW! NOW! NOW! NOW! NOW! NOW! NOW!

SORRY ABOUT YOUR NEW **SNAKE SKIN** BOOTS, BUT **MA** HERE IS **FRIGHTFUL SCARED** OF **SNAKES**!

IT'S NOT HARD, BUT I CAN NEVER
REMEMBER IF I'M SUPPOSE TO GO
AROUND 'EM, OVER 'EM OR AVOID 'EM
COMPLETELY!

DUMB ANIMALS ARE WE? WHAT'S HIS I.Q.?

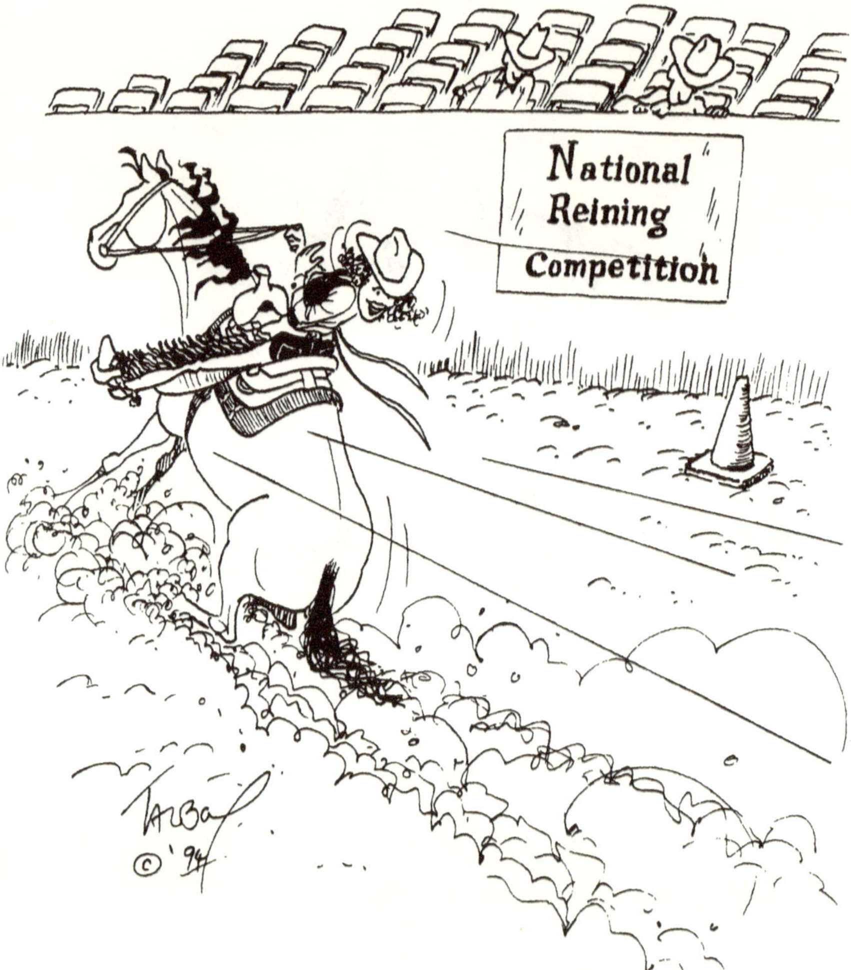
National
Reining
Competition

WOW! LOOK HOW **FAR**
WE **STOPPED**!

OVER-THE-HILL MY FOOT... I'M JUST **MIDDLE-AGED!**

YOU WANT **FENCIN'** LESSONS?
I'LL GIVE YOU **FENCIN'** LESSONS!

WHEN **ROPIN'** GETS IN YOUR
BLOOD ... IT **STAYS** THERE !

RULES?

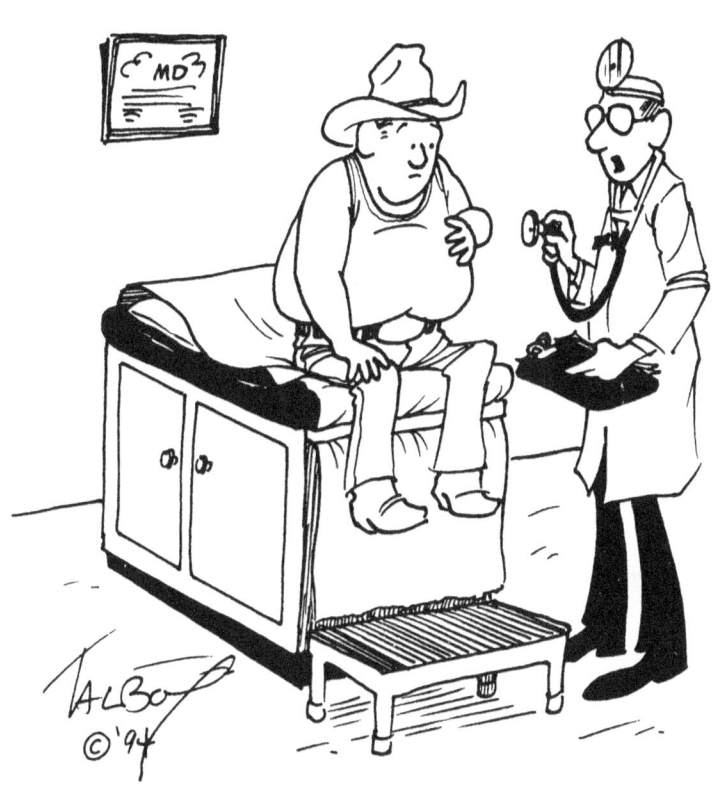

YOU CAN'T LOSE A **MIDDLE-AGE SPREAD** BY SELLING OFF A FEW ACRES!

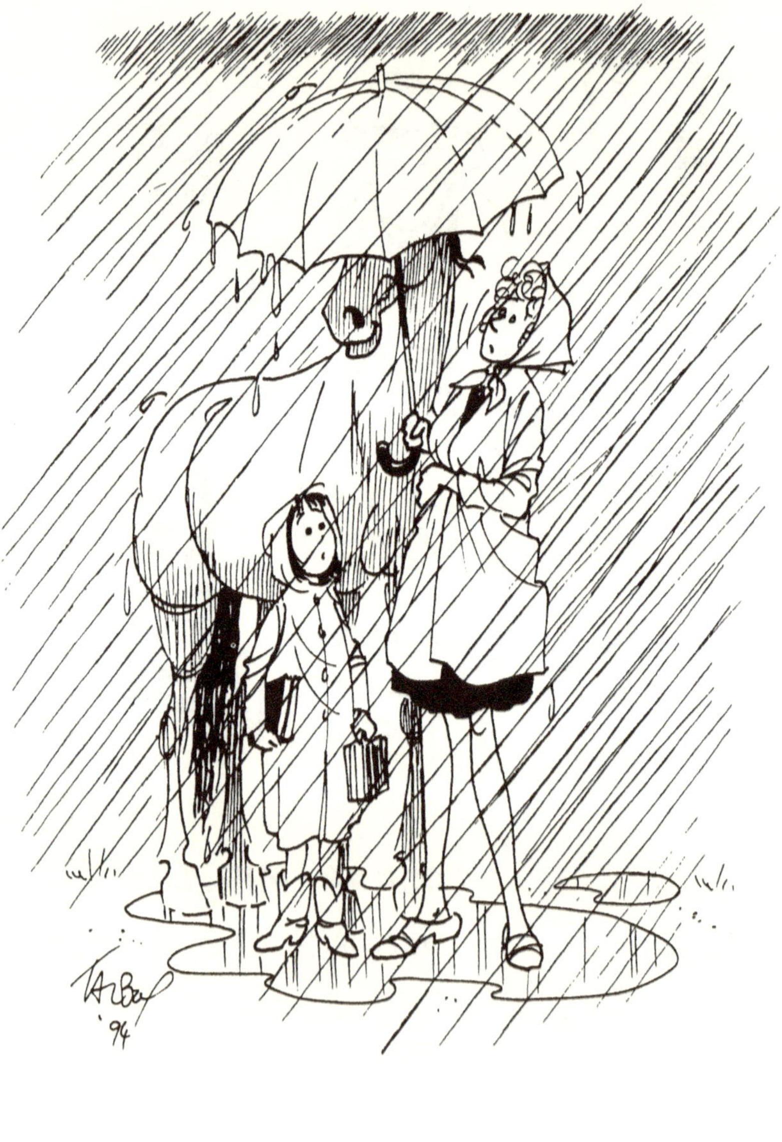

I SEE YALL KNOW THE ROPERS'
SECRET HAND SHAKE! **NO THUMBS!**

BILLY, MY TEACHER SAYS
I'M NOT A COW**GIRL**... I'M
A COW**PERSON**!

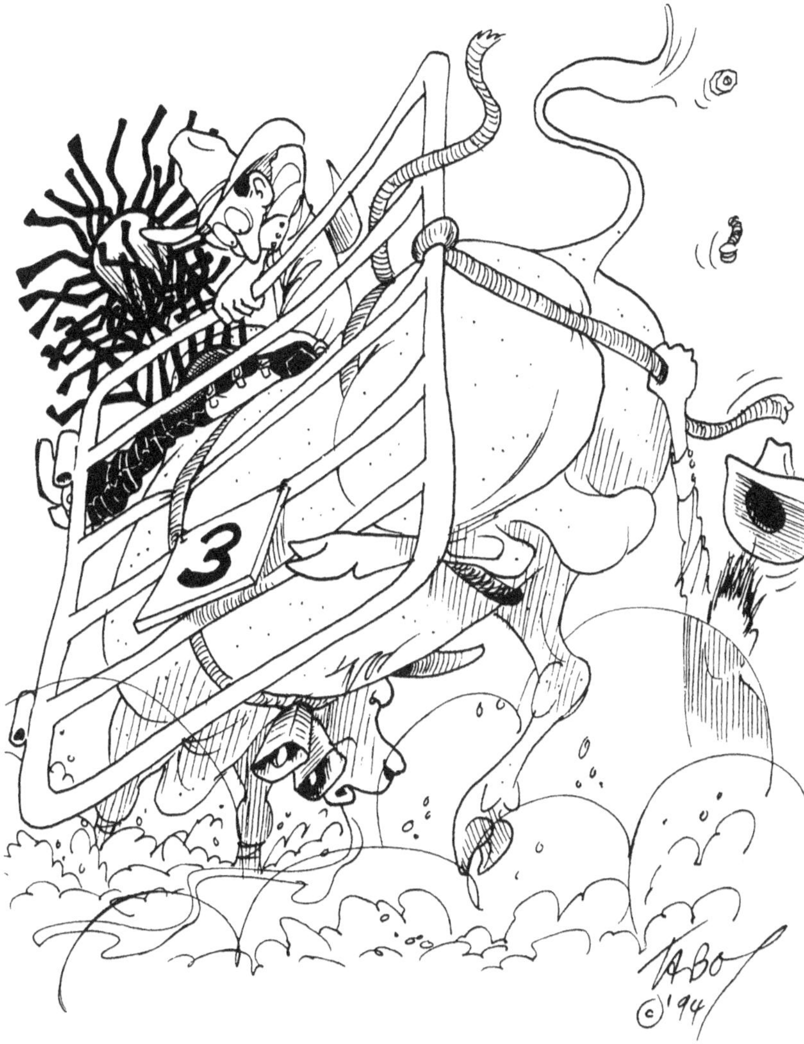
3
©'94

TAKE THE PICTURE! TAKE THE PICTURE!

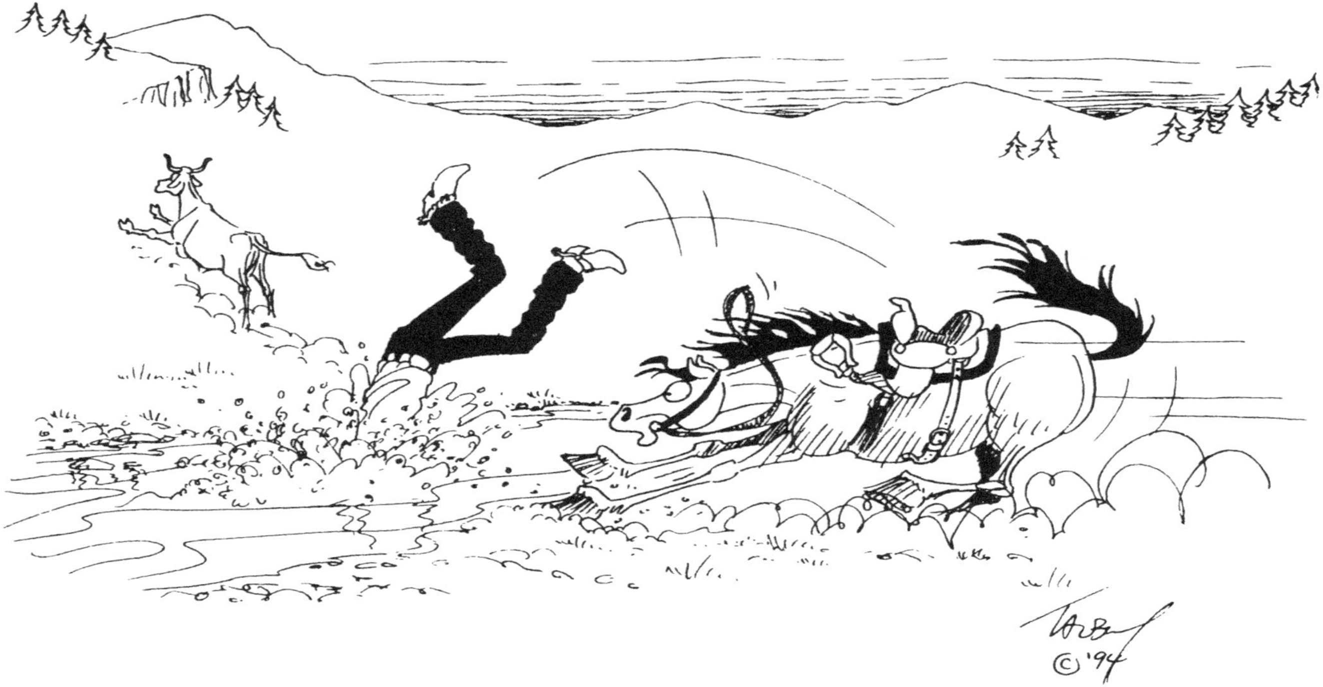

HYDROPHOBIA!

THESE **RANGE** CUBES ARE MADE
BY **ELVES** IN A **HOLLOW TREE**!

BUBBA, DID YOU **DALLY** YOUR **THUMB** AGAIN?

ACTUALLY THIS TRAILOR'S MADE BY **SLINKY**!

LET'S **EAT OUT** TONIGHT!

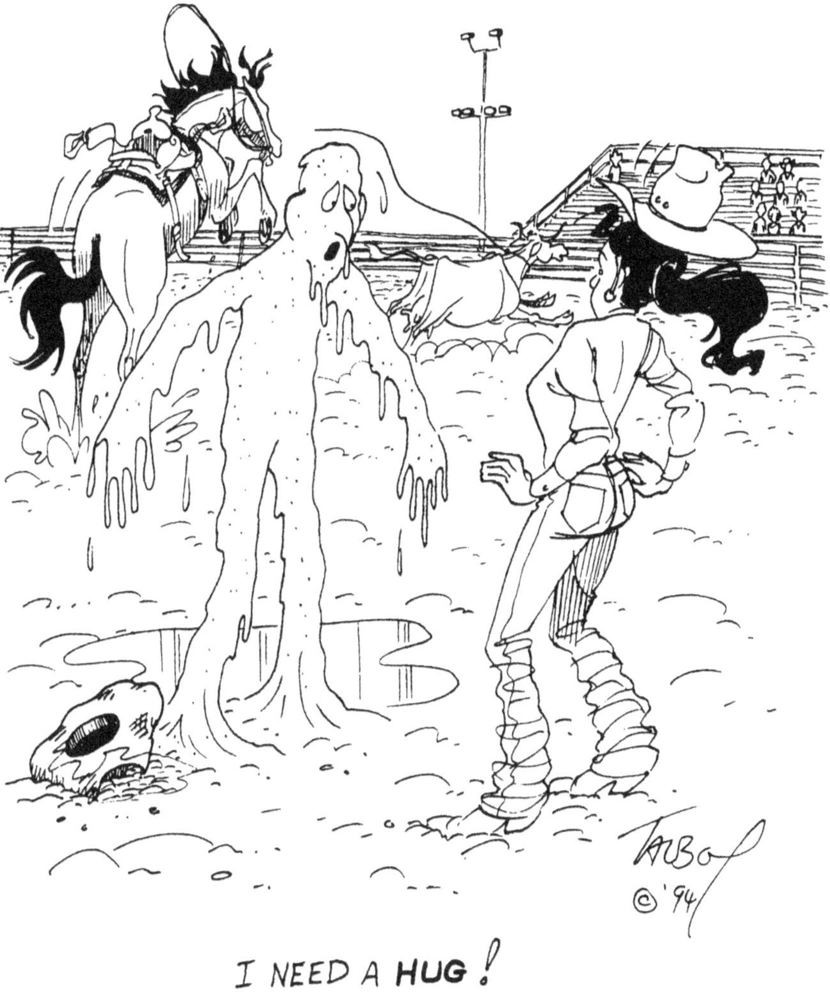
TALBOT
© '94

I NEED A **HUG**!

NO! NO! **SILVER BULLETS** ARE FOR WEREWOLVES!
A STAKE THROUGH THE HEART FOR **VAMPIRES**!
PEOPLE WHO **SNORE** YOU JUST **ROLL OVER**!

HAVE YOU BOYS BEEN **PRACTICIN'** YOUR **ROPIN'** ON THIS COW AGAIN'?

LOSIN' HAIR IS **NOT** A SIGN OF **OLD AGE**... IT'S RIDIN' **FAST** HORSES WITHOUT A **GOOD** HAT !

SORRY, I CAN'T PLAY NOW... I'M
BABYSITTING!

EVER' NOW AN' THEN I HAVE TO PUT
THAT LITTLE **UPSTART** IN HIS PLACE!

COULD YOU SAY A FEW WORDS
TO OUR VIEWING AUDIENCE?

NOW, THAT'S WHAT I CALL
STUBBORN!

The Cartoonist

Daryl Talbot's cowboy cartooning career began with *Western Horseman* magazine in 1965 while he served with the U.S. Marine Corps during the Vietnam era. Later, he won awards for his cartooning while serving as an illustrator in the U.S. Navy. From 1990 to 1992 Daryl exhibited and drew cartoons for rodeo fans and contestants of the National High School Finals Rodeo. This was followed by becoming the "Cowboy Cartoonist Ambassador" for the newly established International Finals Youth Rodeo held each year in Shawnee, Oklahoma. In 1993, Daryl was invited to exhibit his work with a professional cowboy cartoonist group, the Cowboy Cartoonist International, at a special showing in Cody, Wyoming. He was then invited to become a member of the group. In 1994 Daryl was given the honor of being one of five judges in the Miss Rodeo Oklahoma Pageant.

Daryl receives many requests to appear as guest cartoonist at cowboy symposiums, Western festivals, museums, rodeos, and ropings all over the country. He transforms his exhibit into a working studio, and does his cartooning among the people who actually live the cowboy life. Drawing and creating cowboy cartoons while socializing and sharing rodeo and cowboying experiences serves as inspiration for new cartoons. From California to Florida and Texas to Canada, people recognize themselves or their friends in Daryl's cartoons. You often hear comments like "I did that!" "That's so and so!" "That happened to me!" Many of the situations cartooned by Daryl have happened to him, too. Working with his horses and participating in local rodeos have created many humorous, and some not so humorous at the time, predicaments. We've all been there . . . or goin' a be! It's nice to know that you ain't the only one who's "been there and done that."

www.ingramcontent.com/pod-product-compliance
Lightning Source LLC
Chambersburg PA
CBHW020534290526
45786CB00002B/871